Recipes from the Spartan Hunting Preserve

Joy Kemmer

Recipes from the Spartan Hunting Preserve
by Joy Kemmer

ISBN: 978-1-7328283-4-6

Cover Photo: iStockPhoto.com/Polina Lebed

Printed in the United States.

To all the guests who have shared our home, our table, and
our hearts. May your hunt always be blessed.

"Excellent place ... the food and lodging was exceptional ... "

"A great experience! Great food and accommodations and a successful hunt!"

"Mitch and his team make you feel like family and run this place like a well oiled machine. The food is good home cooked meals, the place is kept spotless. I can't wait to book my next trip."

" ... and the meals were fantastic!"

" ... Choosing Spartan Hunting Preserve was the best decision I could have made. The lodge is amazing, The food is some of the best I've ever had. ..."

Contents

Recipe Index

The Spartan Preserve (Food) Story

Hunting and good cooking have always gone hand in hand, and here at the Spartan Hunting Preserve, welcoming hospitality accompanied by hearty appetites and great meals is a given.

Joy Kemmer enjoys a good hunt as much as Mitch, and the two bonded over hunting and other outdoor activities way back in high school. So it stands to reason, Joy also knows her way around the kitchen and enjoys serving up delicious food to welcome the Preserve's many guests.

After numerous requests, she shares her recipes here, in hopes that you'll remember your time at the Lodge fondly, and come back again real soon.

Recipes from the Spartan Hunting Preserve

The Recipes

On the Grill

Grilled Wild Boar Chops

Prep: 15 minutes active plus
Marinate 4 hours
Cook: about 7 minutes
Serves 4

4 wild boar chops
3 lemons, juiced
1 cup olive oil
2 tablespoons olive oil
¼ cup fresh rosemary, chopped
1 tablespoon garlic, minced
1 teaspoon salt, kosher
1 teaspoon black pepper fresh ground

Salt and pepper the chops. Place them in a large non-metal container so each chop lays flat.

Whisk remaining ingredients (except for chops) to make marinade, then pour marinade over the chops. Cover the refrigerate at least four hours, turning every hour or so.

Prepare grill for direct heat on high. Sear chops on both sides for 2 minutes. Turn heat down, or place chops on cooler part of grill for remaining cooking. Close lid and cook about five minutes on each side for medium rare.

Let chops rest at room temp for ten minutes before serving.

Lemon-Herbed Fallow Deer Filet and Vegetables

Serves: 4

Four 4- oz. Fallow Deer filets
2 tablespoons butter, melted
1 tablespoon fresh lemon juice
Salt, to taste
1 package (1 lb) frozen vegetable medley (broccoli, cauliflower and carrots)
2 cloves garlic, minced
2 teaspoons grated lemon peel
1 teaspoon dried thyme leaves
¼ teaspoon pepper

In small bowl, combine seasoning ingredients; mix well. Remove 1 tablespoon seasoning; press remaining seasoning mixture evenly into both sides of Fallow Deer filets.

Stir melted butter, lemon juice and ¼ teaspoon salt into reserved tablespoon of seasoning, set aside.

Place filets on grill over medium coals. Grill, uncovered, 2-3 minutes per side, turning once. Since Fallow Deer is naturally low in fat, it is best not to overcook as it tends to dry out.

Meanwhile, prepare vegetables according to package directions. Combine vegetables and lemon butter seasoning mixture; toss to coat.

After letting filets rest for 10 minutes, carve crosswise into thick slices; season with salt as desired. Serve with vegetables.

Soups & Stews

Potato - Spartan Sausage Barley Soup

Prep: 10 minutes
Cook: 30 minutes
Serves: 12 (4 qt.)

1 ½ lbs. Spartan Sausage
1 large green pepper, chopped
7 cups chicken broth
1 package (32 oz.) frozen cubed hash brown potatoes
1 can (28 oz.) crushed tomatoes, undrained
2 tablespoons reduced - sodium soy sauce
2 ½ teaspoon garlic powder
2 ½ teaspoon dried thyme
1 ½ teaspoon pepper
1 can (16 oz.) cut green beans
½ cup quick-cooking barley

Spray a large Dutch with cooking spray, cook Spartan Sausage and green pepper over medium heat until meat is no longer pink; drain.

Stir in water, potatoes, tomatoes, soy sauce, garlic powder, thyme, salt and pepper. Bring to a boil. Reduce heat; cover and simmer for 10-15 minutes or until potatoes are tender.

Return to a boil; stir in green beans and barley.

Reduce heat; cover and simmer for 10-12 minutes or until beans and barley are tender.
Remove from the heat; let stand for five minutes, and serve.

Spartan Sausage and Cheese Soup

Prep: 45 minutes
Cook: 10 minutes
Serves: 8

½ lb. Spartan Sausage
4 tablespoons butter, divided
¾ cup chopped onion
¾ cup shredded carrots
¾ cup diced celery
1 teaspoon dried basil
1 teaspoon dried parsley flakes

1 ¾ lbs. (about 4 cups) cubed peeled potatoes
3 cups chicken broth
¼ cup all-purpose flour
1 pkg. (16 oz.) Velveeta process cheese, cubed
1 ¾ cups whole milk
¾ to ½ teaspoon salt
¼ cup sour cream

In a large saucepan over medium heat, cook and crumble Spartan Sausage until no longer pink; drain and set aside. In same saucepan, melt 1 tablespoon butter over medium heat.

Sauté onion, carrots, celery, basil and parsley until tender, about 10 minutes.

Add the potatoes, Spartan Sausage and broth; bring to a boil. Reduce heat and simmer, covered, until potatoes are tender, 10 - 12 minutes.

Meanwhile, in a small skillet, melt remaining butter. Add flour; cook and stir until bubbly, 3 - 5 minutes.

Add to soup; bring to a boil. Cook and stir 2 minutes.

Reduce heat to low. Stir in cheese, milk, salt and pepper; cook until cheese melts. Remove from heat; blend in sour cream.

Pizza Soup

Prep: 15 minutes
Cook: 20 minutes
Serves: 6

1 lb. Spartan Sausage
1 small onion, chopped
1 cup sliced fresh mushrooms
1 medium green pepper, cut into strips
1 can (28 oz.) diced tomatoes, undrained
1 cup beef broth
1 cup sliced pepperoni
1 teaspoon dried basil
shredded mozzarella cheese

In a large saucepan, cook the Spartan Sausage, onion, mushrooms and green pepper over medium heat until meat is no longer pink and vegetables are almost tender; drain.

Stir in the tomatoes, broth, pepperoni and basil. Cook until heated through.

Ladle into oven-proof bowls; top each with desired amount of cheese. Broil or microwave until cheese melts and is bubbly. Serve hot.

Spartan Sausage Stuffed Pepper Soup

Prep: 10 minutes
Cook: 30 minutes

1 tablespoon olive oil
1 lb. Spartan Sausage
¾ cup chopped onions
1 ½ teaspoons minced garlic
Salt and pepper to taste
1 red bell pepper, cut into ½-inch pieces
1 green bell pepper, cut into ½-inch pieces

1 14.5-ounce can petite diced tomatoes
1 15-ounce can tomato sauce
1 14.5-ounce can beef broth
2 teaspoons Italian seasoning
2 cups cooked white rice
2 tablespoons freshly chopped parsley

Heat the olive oil in a large pot over medium high heat. Add the Spartan Sausage and cook until browned, breaking up into smaller pieces with a spatula (approximately 5-6 minutes).

Add the onion and cook for 4-5 minutes or until softened. Add the garlic and cook for 30 seconds.

Season the Spartan Sausage and onion mixture with salt and pepper. Add the bell peppers to the pot and cook for 2-3 minutes.

Add the tomatoes, tomato sauce, beef broth and Italian seasoning to the pot; bring to a simmer. Cook for 15-20 minutes or until peppers are tender.

Stir in the rice and season the soup with salt and pepper to taste. Sprinkle with parsley and serve.

Spartan Sausage and Vegetable Soup

Prep: 20 minutes
Cook: 40 minutes

2 teaspoons of olive oil
½ cup of onions finely diced
2 carrots peeled, quartered and sliced
2 stalks celery thinly sliced
1 lb. of Spartan Sausage
2 teaspoons minced garlic
Salt and pepper to taste
1 15-ounce can of diced tomatoes (do not drain)
1 8-ounce can of tomato sauce

1 teaspoon of Italian seasoning (or equal parts of garlic powder, dried oregano and dried basil)
6 cups of beef broth
1 large russet potato, peeled and diced into ½-inch cubes
½ cup frozen corn
½ cup diced green beans
2 tablespoons of chopped fresh parsley

Heat the olive oil in a large pot over medium high heat. Add onion, carrots and celery to the pot. Cook for 5-6 minutes or until soft.

Add the Spartan Sausage and season with salt and pepper to taste. Cook, breaking up the Spartan Sausage with a spoon, until browned and mostly cooked through. Add garlic and cook for 30 seconds more.

Add tomatoes, tomato sauce, Italian seasoning, beef broth and potato to the pot; bring to a simmer.

Cook for 25-30 minutes more, or until potatoes are tender. Taste and add salt and pepper as desired. Stir in corn and green beans and cook for 5 minutes more. Sprinkle with parsley and serve.

Broccoli-Chicken Rice Soup

Prep: 30 minutes
Serves: 6

4 cups whole milk
2 cans (14 ½ oz. each) chicken broth
1 envelope ranch salad dressing mix
2 cups fresh broccoli florets
½ lb. process cheese (shredded cheese)
3 cups cooked rice
2 cups cubed cooked chicken

Combine milk, broth, and dressing mix in a large soup pan and bring to a boil.

Add broccoli and cook, uncovered, until tender.

Stir in cheese until melted.

Add cooked rice and chicken. Heat through. Serve hot.

Brown Rice Chicken Soup

Prep: 30 minutes
Serves: 5

1 cup diced sweet red pepper
½ cup chopped onions
½ cup sliced celery
1 can diced carrots
2 garlic cloves, minced
2 tablespoons of butter
3 cans (14 ½ oz. each) reduced sodium chicken broth
1 teaspoon dried thyme
¼ teaspoon pepper
2 cups cubed cooked chicken breast
1 cup instant brown rice
¼ cup sliced green onions

Sauté pepper, onion, celery, and garlic in butter until veggies are tender.

Add broth, thyme, and pepper. Bring to a boil.

Reduce heat, cover, and simmer for 5 minutes.

Stir in chicken and rice; bring to a boil. Then simmer uncovered for 5 minutes until rice is tender.

Macaroni & Cheese Soup with Broccoli & Chicken

1 yellow bell pepper
1 onion
2 boxes Mac and Cheese
chicken tenderloin pieces, chopped small
2 cups milk
2 cups half & half
1 can of Campbell Cheddar Cheese soup
2 cups broccoli
salt and pepper to taste
garlic salt to taste

Chop pepper and onion and sauté.

Add cut up chicken and cook.

Separately, cook Mac and Cheese as directed on the box.

Cook broccoli until soft.

Add all ingredients together. Serve hot.

Barbeque Chicken Soup

2 cups cooked and shredded chicken tenderloin
spice mixture including: minced garlic, garlic powder, onion powder, and black pepper to suit
8 cups chicken broth
1 ½ cups barbeque sauce
2 15-ounce cans sweet corn
1 15-ounce can cannelloni white beans

Mix all ingredients together and heat through.

Garnish with cheese. Serve with tortilla chips if desired.

Shrimp and Crab Soup

1 lb. of shrimp
1 lb. of crab meat
2 cans cream style corn
2 cans cream of potato soup
1 quart half & half
1 ½ sticks butter
2 tablespoons flour
salt and pepper to taste
1 onion, diced

Saute onion in butter. Stir in flour and cook a couple of minutes.

Add soup and corn and cook until bubbly.

Then add crab, shrimp, half & half, salt, and pepper.

Reduce heat to low and simmer until cook through and flavors blend. Do not boil. Serve hot.

Cream of Crab Soup

1 onion, diced
1 green bell pepper, diced
4 Tablespoons butter or oil
1 Tablespoon garlic

1 large can of cream of chicken soup
1 small can of cheddar cheese soup
4 cups of half & half
2 to 3 cups of chicken broth
1 can corn kernels
1 large bag frozen shredded hash brown style potatoes
2 packages crab meat, finely shredded
salt, pepper, and Old Bay seasoning as desired

Sauté onion, bell pepper, garlic and butter together.

Then add remaining ingredients.

Stir until warm and bubbly, then serve.

Spartan Fallow Deer Stew

1 onion, diced
3 stalks celery, diced
2 tablespoons oil
1 to 1 ½ lbs Fallow Deer meat, cubed
salt and pepper to taste
1 (30-oz) can tomato sauce with Italian herbs
3 bay leaves
1 can corn kernels
1 can green beans
2 (30 oz) cans Homestyle Veg-All large cut vegetables
Chicken broth

Sauté onion and celery in oil.

Add Fallow Deer meat, salt and pepper and cook on low heat until meat is mostly cooked through.

Next add tomato sauce and bay leaves. Continue cooking for a few minutes.

Add corn, green beans, and vegetables, along with chicken broth to bring stew to desired consistency.

Simmer about 30 minutes more, remove bay leaves, and serve.

Spartan Chili

1 lb. Spartan Sausage
1 large onion, diced
1 green pepper, diced
1 tablespoon olive oil
salt and pepper
chili powder
cumin
Worcestershire sauce
A-1 Steak Sauce
1 15-oz. can tomato sauce
1 30-oz can Bush's Chili Beans
1 15-oz can Bush's Black Beans
1 15-oz can Bush's Cannelloni Beans
chicken broth

Saute Spartan Sausage with onion, green pepper, and olive oil.

Add salt, pepper, chili powder and cumin to your personal preference.

Add Worcestershire Sauce and A1 Steak Sauce to your personal preference, and tomato sauce.

Stir well to mix. Then add beans, and chicken broth to bring the chili to your desired consistency.

Simmer 15 minutes more to allow flavors to blend before serving.

From the Oven

Spartan Pork Roast

Spartan Pork Roast
1 packet dry onion soup mix
1 packet brown gravy mix
garlic salt, to taste

Place Spartan Pork Roast in a slow cooker. Top with soup and gravy mixes.

Also sprinkle with garlic salt or any desired spices.

Pour enough water over the top to fill almost half way up the Roast. Cover and cook on low setting (around 250 degrees) for 8 to 11 hours, depending on the size of the roast.

Cook until meat tears away from the bone easily.

Pulled Spartan Pork Barbecue

leftovers from Spartan Pork Roast recipe (page 33)
barbeque sauce
seasoned salt or garlic salt
chicken broth

After serving Spartan Pork Roast, take any leftover Roast Meat and shred it. Remove excess fat and bones.

Then simmer with barbeque sauce.

Add seasoned salt and/or garlic salt along with a bit of chicken broth if desired.

Fallow Deer Roast

Serves 6.

3 lb. Fallow Deer Roast
6 potatoes, peeled and quartered
2 tablespoons cooking oil
1 stalk celery, chopped
1 bay leaf
1 cup apple juice
1 teaspoon salt
1 cup water
6 peppercorns
½ teaspoon pepper
4 carrots, sliced
1 tablespoon cornstarch
6 Spanish onions

Pre-heat oven to 300 degrees. Heat oil over medium heat. Add Fallow Deer roast and brown well on all sides.

Add onions, carrots, celery, bay leaf, salt, pepper, apple juice and water. Cover and place in preheated oven for 1 hour.

Remove from oven, add potatoes. Cover and return to oven for 1 hour or until potatoes are fork tender. Thicken gravy with cornstarch.

Roasted Fallow Deer in Beer Sauce

Serves 4

1 3 - 4 lb. Fallow Roast or chuck
1 onion, sliced
½ cup chili sauce
2 tablespoons brown sugar
1 or more cloves garlic
12 oz. beer, more if necessary
salt and pepper to taste

Place the roast in a 9 x 13" baking dish. Cover with onion rings.

In a bowl, combine chili sauce, brown sugar, garlic and beer, then pour over meat.

Cover and bake at 350 degrees for 3 ½ to 4 hours.

Note: Leftovers are delicious in sandwiches with barbeque sauce.

Spartan Fallow Deer Meatballs

Serves 4

Meatballs:
2 lbs. ground Fallow Deer burger
2 eggs, beaten
1 cup bread crumbs
1 pkg. Lipton Onion Soup Mix

Sauce:
1 can sauerkraut (large, rinsed once)
1 can whole cranberries in cranberry sauce
1 jar chili sauce
1 cup brown sugar

To make meatballs, preheat oven to 350 degrees. Mix ingredients, roll into bit-size meatballs. Place in 9 x 12" pan, set aside.

Prepare sauce: in a separate bowl, mix all ingredients. Pour over meatballs.

Bake 1 ½ hours stirring once after 1 hour, and again when done. Serve warm with toothpicks.

Rice & Pasta

Spartan Dirty Rice

3 tablespoons olive oil
1 onion, diced
3 cloves garlic
1 green pepper, diced
1 lb. Spartan Sausage
salt and pepper
1 yellow or red bell pepper, diced
2 tablespoons Tony Cachery's seasoning
3 bay leaves
3 cups cooked rice
chicken broth

Sauté oil, peppers, onion, and garlic a few minutes. Then add Spartan Sausage and all seasonings and bay leaves. Cook until sausage is browned.

Add chicken broth and cooked rice to desired consistency.
Simmer until ready to serve.

Spartan Sausage Spaghetti Sauce

1 diced onion
2 cloves of garlic
1/8 cup olive oil
salt and pepper
1 green pepper, diced
1 lb. of Spartan Sausage
basil
oregano
1 extra large container spaghetti sauce
1 can diced mushrooms
1 can black olives
3 tablespoons brown sugar

Sauté oil, onions, pepper and garlic a few minutes. Add sausage, all seasonings, and cook until sausage is brown. Then add sauce, mushrooms, black olives, and brown sugar.

Reduce heat to low, simmer to desired consistency.

Macaroni and Cheese with Spartan Sausage

1 lb. Spartan Sausage
1 onion, chopped
1 teaspoon garlic
1 box Mac and Cheese
1 can green beans
1 can whole kernel sweet corn
1 can sliced carrots
oregano
garlic salt
salt and pepper

Sauté garlic and onion for a few minutes to soften. Add Spartan Sausage and cook until browned.

Prepare Mac and Cheese according to directions on box, then add all ingredients to it.

Spartan Sausage Pasta e Fagioli

Prep: 40 minutes
Serves 24 (7 ½ qt)

2 lbs Spartan Sausage
6 cans (14 ½ oz. each) beef broth
2 cans (28 oz. each) diced tomatoes, undrained
2 jars (26 oz. each) spaghetti sauce
3 large onions, chopped
8 celery ribs, diced
3 medium carrots, sliced
2 cups canned cannellini beans, rinsed and drained
2 cups canned kidney beans, rinsed and drained
3 teaspoons minced fresh oregano or 1 teaspoon dried oregano
2 ½ teaspoons pepper
1 ½ teaspoon hot pepper sauce
8 oz uncooked medium pasta shells
5 teaspoons minced fresh parsley

In a large stockpot, cook Spartan Sausage over medium heat until no longer pink; drain.

Add broth, tomatoes, spaghetti sauce, onions, celery, carrots, beans, oregano, pepper and pepper sauce.

Bring to a boil, then, reduce heat; simmer, covered, 30 minutes. Add pasta and parsley; simmer, covered, 10 - 14 minutes or until pasta is tender.

The Spartan Hunting Preserve

The Kemmer Family came to historic Grassy Cove Tennessee in 1806. Mitch Kemmer's grandfather, due to an Air Force career, was moved to Gulfport Mississippi. Here his father, Norman Kemmer, took up hog hunting in the swamps and bayous of the deep south. He became renowned throughout the hog hunting communities for, not only his hog hunting knowledge, but also his extremely tough line of catch dogs. He began this line of dogs in the mid 1960's. After forty years of selective breeding these dogs are known around the world for their grit and determination. These same dogs make up the hog catching staff, when needed, at the Spartan Hunting Preserve.

As for the location dogs, or bay dogs, we look to another famous dog man in the Kemmer Family. Robert Kemmer still maintains a line of cur dogs that have been in the Kemmer family since their arrival in Grassy Cove in 1806. Kemmer Curs are world famous for their hunting skills. (Mitch and his father were Elk hunting in the Selway-Bitterroot Wilderness in Idaho in 1999. While there, they passed a Montana hunter who had a sign on his truck that read, "I hunt Kemmer Curs.") These are the same curs, when needed, that will be used to locate your Trophy Boar at Spartan Hunting Preserve.

When you come to this Preserve you will be entering a family operated business. Robert Kemmer lives only a few miles from the Preserve and has been involved and consulted throughout its conception. Robert guided and organized hunts for the Historic Renegade Hunting Lodge for years. Thanks to him, Mitch has been in the hog woods practically since birth. When he was five years old, his parents took him hog hunting in Chalmette Louisiana and they caught 10 boars and brought them out alive. These are the kind of stories that have always made up his life, and he considers himself to be a truly blessed man. When you come here you will receive personal attention from the Kemmer Family doing what we have done for generations.

Find us at **BoarHuntingTN.com** or on Facebook at **facebook.com/spartanpreserve**

About the Author

Joy Mitchell Kemmer has a Bachelors Degree in Nutrition from Berea College in Kentucky. She married Mitch in 2000 in Tennessee and they were farming and raising children. She fed her large family many wild game dishes after hunts with Mitch and they grew in popularity. After opening Spartan Hunting Preserve in 2008 she offered many dishes to the guests at the Lodge that soon became requested favorites. Some of the recipes featured here have been contributed by other extended family as well as frequent clients at the Lodge. The 'Joy' of food is sharing it with loved ones and we hope some of these meals can bless your family too.

Lightning Source UK Ltd.
Milton Keynes UK
UKHW051110070621
384904UK00012B/703